Original title:
Refractions of the Starlit Path

Copyright © 2025 Swan Charm
All rights reserved.

Author: Sabrina Sarvik
ISBN HARDBACK: 978-1-80565-099-7
ISBN PAPERBACK: 978-1-80565-302-8

Pilgrimage to the Heart of the Cosmos

Beneath the vast, unfathomed skies,
A journey starts where starlight lies.
With souls entwined in cosmic flight,
We seek the heart, a glowing light.

Through galaxies of swirling haze,
We dance through time in endless ways.
Each step we take, a tale unfolds,
Of wonders deep and dreams of gold.

Our hearts beat soft, a rhythmic sound,
In realms where magic can be found.
With every breath, the universe sighs,
As ancient truths begin to rise.

In whispers carried on the breeze,
We find our path through astral seas.
To know the songs of stars above,
Is to embrace the pulse of love.

So side by side, we journey forth,
In search of wisdom, timeless worth.
With hearts as one, we'll find our trace,
A pilgrimage to cosmic grace.

Whispers of Celestial Light

In shadows soft, the echoes call,
Of starlight whispers, gentle, small.
Through velvet nights, in silence steep,
The secrets of the heavens creep.

Each twinkle bright a story spun,
Of dreams alight from moonlit sun.
With open hearts, we hear their song,
A melody where we belong.

Through twilight veils, the cosmos gleams,
As if revealing hidden dreams.
A tapestry of light unfurled,
Connecting every boy and girl.

In silence sweet, the stars align,
Their laughter bright, a sacred sign.
In every shimmer, hope ignites,
Through whispers of celestial lights.

So close your eyes and feel the glow,
Of ancient tales that ebb and flow.
Embrace the night with joy and grace,
In whispered dance, we find our place.

Dances Beneath the Canopy of Stars

Beneath the canopy so wide,
We spin in circles, side by side.
With every twirl, the heavens gleam,
A universe of shared dreams.

The moon above casts silver beams,
As we weave in sync with dreams.
The stars, they wink and gently sway,
Inviting us to join their play.

In harmony, our spirits rise,
As constellations fill the skies.
We laugh and twirl, a joyful choir,
Our hearts ablaze with cosmic fire.

Through night's embrace, we lose our fear,
For every star brings dreams more near.
With hands held high, we greet the light,
In dances bold, we claim the night.

So let us twirl beneath the glow,
Where cosmic rhythms gently flow.
In harmony with starry arts,
We dance beneath the night with hearts.

Glimmers on the Midnight Trail

As shadows deepen, night unfolds,
The midnight trail with secrets holds.
In hushed embrace, the world grows still,
A guiding light, a whispered will.

With every step on path so worn,
Glimmers appear, a new dawn's born.
The stars, like lanterns, guide our way,
Illuminating the dreams we sway.

Each glimmer speaks of tales untold,
Of journeys brave, of hearts so bold.
In every flicker, hope ignites,
As we traverse those enchanted nights.

Through tangled woods and silver streams,
The midnight trail fulfills our dreams.
With every heartbeat, truth revealed,
Our destinies, the stars have sealed.

So trust the glimmers, follow true,
In every shadow, light shines through.
On paths unknown, we find our song,
In midnight's glow, where we belong.

The Alchemy of Night's Illumination

In silver whispers, shadows play,
The stars begin to weave their sway.
A tapestry of dreams unfolds,
As secrets of the night are told.

With each flicker, the worlds collide,
In moonlit realms where hopes abide.
The alchemist's hand turns lead to gold,
Transforming tales of lives untold.

Through azure depths, the echoes soar,
While night unveils its hidden lore.
A symphony of light's embrace,
In realms where time and space interlace.

In quiet corners, lovers sigh,
Their dreams take wing, as stars comply.
Each pulse of light, a fragile thread,
Connecting hearts where angels tread.

The night, a canvas dark and bright,
The unseen dance of day and night.
With every glow, a spark ignites,
Unraveling the world's delights.

Lanterns of Thought Adrift in the Midnight Glow

In twilight's hush, the lanterns gleam,
Weighty thoughts like paper dreams.
They float and drift on midnight's tide,
While mysteries dance, they softly bide.

Each flicker shines, a beckoning spark,
Guiding the mind through the deep, dark.
With whispers low, they cast their nets,
Capturing hopes as dusk begets.

Through murky depths, the truths emerge,
With every heartbeat, doubts converge.
On feathered wings of night's embrace,
Each lantern glows with gentle grace.

Adrift among shadows, thoughts entwine,
In midnight's quilt, where stars align.
Their glow ignites a path unknown,
Illuminating the heart's own throne.

So let them drift, these lanterns bright,
Through velvet skies of endless night.
They carry dreams to shores unseen,
In the tapestry of what has been.

The Unseen Threads of a Celestial Dance

Oh, celestial tapestry, finely spun,
In cosmic silence, our fates are won.
Through heartbeats synced with distant stars,
Each thread of light tells tales of ours.

The moonlight weaves through time's embrace,
As constellations share their grace.
In shadows soft, the secrets seethe,
Binding lives in twilight's breathe.

With every twirl, the cosmos sighs,
The stardust whispers, never lies.
Waltzing through the velvet night,
Unseen threads bring forth the light.

In gentle spirals, dreams take flight,
A grand ballet in the soft twilight.
While each star glimmers, a wish is sown,
In the vast expanse, we are not alone.

For every heart holds cosmic sway,
In this grand dance, we find our way.
Entwined in mysteries, lost in chance,
Together we join the celestial dance.

Mysterious Shadows beneath Cosmic Canopies

Beneath the vast and starry skies,
Where ancient wisdom softly lies.
The shadows stretch like whispered lore,
Inviting souls to seek and explore.

In twilight's grasp, the secrets creep,
While silver dreams in stillness seep.
A cosmic dance of ebb and flow,
In ways unknown, the heartbeats grow.

Through nebulous realms, the echoes call,
Offering solace to one and all.
In shadows deep, the mysteries weave,
A promise for those who dare to believe.

Mysterious whispers in the dark,
Where tales of wonder leave their mark.
Under canopies of twinkling night,
We find our paths, led by soft light.

So roam the depths of cosmic dreams,
In shadows dance, where starlight gleams.
For within the veils of the vast unknown,
Our spirits thrive, forever grown.

An Odyssey through the Night's Embrace

Beneath the moon's soft, silver glow,
Whispers linger where shadows flow.
Upon the path where dreams take flight,
We wander forth through the deepening night.

Stars caress the velvet sky,
Echoes of laughter swirling high.
With each step, magic blooms and twirls,
As hearts entwine in this world of pearls.

In the hush, secrets gently stir,
Woven tales in the softest purr.
The night, a canvas of infinite hue,
Brushes our souls in whispers anew.

With eyes aglow, we delve deep still,
Chasing the whispers, the ancient thrill.
For every wanderer finds their way,
In night's embrace, where dreams sway.

And as the dawn begins to creep,
We hold the magic, a treasure to keep.
In hearts and minds, the journey stays,
An odyssey woven in night's warm gaze.

Wandering Souls in Night's Fold

In the stillness where shadows creep,
Wandering souls, secrets they keep.
Underneath the tapestry of stars,
They trace the echoes of long-lost scars.

With every breath, the night unfolds,
Fables of ancient love retold.
The gentle breeze, a lover's sigh,
Calls to the dreamers who wish to fly.

Moonlit paths, a dance of grace,
Leading our hearts to a distant place.
Through whispered wishes and silken dreams,
The sky adorned with silver beams.

Lost in the beauty of night's embrace,
Time slows down in this sacred space.
Each heartbeat syncs with the stars above,
In the fold of night, we find our love.

And when the dawn begins to glow,
The wanderers rise, ready to go.
Yet the solace of night will forever bind,
Wandering souls, to the dreams they find.

Celestial Journeys through Twilight's Gaze

In twilight's arms, dreams take flight,
Whirling softly in the dimming light.
The cosmos beckons, a siren song,
Guiding us where we all belong.

Every star holds a tale unfurled,\nA piece of hope in this vast world.
Through celestial pathways, we chase the dawn,
On wings of wonder, we are reborn.

With every flicker, a heartbeat beats,
In the quiet, the universe greets.
A tapestry spun of moments bright,
Guiding us through the veil of night.

Through starlit whispers, we intertwine,
In this timeless dance, where spirits shine.
Each journey, a myriad of delight,
Celestial dreams take shape in flight.

As morning weaves its golden thread,
We treasure the paths where our hearts have led.
In the glow of day, we'll softly gaze,
At celestial journeys through twilight's haze.

Luminous Dreams of Enchanted Nights

In the hush of night, dreams softly rise,
Luminous whispers beneath starry skies.
Magic dances in the cool, crisp air,
Awakening wonders, beyond compare.

With each heartbeat, the world transforms,
Into a realm where enchantment warms.
Fairy tales spun in the silken breeze,
Wrap us in wonders, as spirits tease.

Under the gaze of the watchful moon,
Every heart hums a familiar tune.
In enchanted corners where shadows play,
Luminous dreams guide us on our way.

The night unfolds with stories profound,
Colors bursting where magic is found.
We drift through realms draped in delight,
In luminous dreams of enchanted night.

And when the dawn calls, soft and bright,
We'll carry the glow from the starlit night.
For deep in our hearts, forever stays,
The magic of dreams and enchanted ways.

Astral Brushstrokes on a Canvas of Dark

In the canvas where shadows dance,
Stars ignite with a fleeting glance.
Brushstrokes weave the nightingale's song,
Whispers of dreams where the lost belong.

Colors blend in hues of delight,
Painting tales in the quiet night.
Each stroke a tale, each twist a turn,
In silent corners, the heavens burn.

Mysteries spin in the ink-black sky,
Wandering souls and wishes fly.
The universe hums a soft refrain,
Celestial secrets to entertain.

A cosmic dance of fate and desire,
Sparks of magic that never tire.
With every night the stories grow,
In the dark, the lights overflow.

Here, in shadows, the dreams awake,
Heartfelt wishes as moments break.
The canvas shimmers, painted true,
A night sky kissed by vibrant hue.

The Labyrinth of Light Beneath the Stars

Within the maze where shadows meander,
Glow of lanterns beckons to wander.
Footsteps echo on the cobblestone,
Lost in the brilliance, forever alone.

Twists and turns where the echoes call,
Guiding the heart when it fears to fall.
Alive with whispers of stories old,
Where light unfolds, and dreams are bold.

Each corner holds fragments of time,
Stories entwined in rhythm and rhyme.
Beneath the stars, the path is clear,
A symphony of what we hold dear.

Hope glimmers softly on the breeze,
As life unfolds with graceful ease.
In the labyrinth, every soul finds light,
Embracing shadows that dance in the night.

Through the darkness, we bravely roam,
Finding the paths that lead us home.
With each step, our spirits soar,
In this maze of stars, forevermore.

Celestial Breezes and Gentle Whispers

On gentle wings, the breezes glide,
Carrying secrets of the night wide.
Whispers weave through the velvet skies,
Tales of joy, and soft goodbyes.

Stars align in a cosmic thread,
Sowing dreams in the hearts widespread.
Where thoughts take flight on fleeting sighs,
Cradled softly, where starlight lies.

Every breeze a lullaby sweet,
In moonlight's arms, our souls will meet.
Messages wrapped in silken air,
Binding us close, with tender care.

Through celestial paths, we float and spin,
Finding solace where the night begins.
An orchestra of light, soft and rare,
Stars hum gently, lost in the air.

In cosmic corners, our hearts ignite,
United as one under starry night.
Breezes carry our hopes with grace,
In gentle whispers, we find our place.

Flickers of Hope in the Abyss of Night

In the depths where darkness resides,
Flickers of hope in silence abides.
Glimmers dance on the edge of despair,
Painting the shadows with colors rare.

Each spark a promise, a beacon bright,
Guiding our hearts through the long, cold night.
In the void where our fears collide,
A flame ignites, where dreams abide.

Through the silence, our spirits rise,
Shattering doubts with resolute cries.
For every star that fades from view,
A thousand more begin anew.

In the abyss, we learn to fight,
Finding courage under the night.
Hope glows softly, a tender flame,
Whispering softly, it calls our name.

Beyond the dark, the dawn will break,
A testament of all we stake.
In the night, when shadows loom,
Flickers of hope will always bloom.

Beneath the Cloak of Cosmic Wonders

In shadows deep, where secrets lie,
The whispers of the stars drift by.
With stardust dreams and glimmering light,
We wander through the endless night.

The universe sprawls, an ancient quilt,
Of tales and fables, softly built.
Each twinkle tells of journeys far,
A cosmic dance, a silent spar.

Beneath the cloak of velvet skies,
Our spirits soar, our minds arise.
We trace the paths of fading suns,
In this vast realm where time outruns.

Galaxies swirl in a lover's embrace,
As we explore this sacred space.
With every heartbeat, wonder grows,
In the garden where creation flows.

So let us bask in twilight's grace,
And find our place in this vast race.
For beneath the cosmic wonders' crest,
We seek the truth, we seek the best.

A Symphony of Stars and Silhouettes

In the night, a melody plays,
A symphony of endless days.
The stars join in with shimmering notes,
While shadows dance in endless moats.

Each twinkling light, a voice so pure,
Echoing stories, both bright and obscure.
With every breath, the night weaves sound,
In rhythms soft, our hearts are bound.

Silhouettes move in the soft moonlight,
Creating figures that take to flight.
They spin and sway like willow trees,
Dancing gently in the evening breeze.

The cosmos hums a timeless tune,
With harmony bright beneath the moon.
In this vast orchestra of the skies,
We lose ourselves, and the world flies.

For in this dance of stars and night,
We find our souls take glorious flight.
In the symphony, we are entwined,
With every heartbeat, fate designed.

Dancing Along the Milky Way's Edge

On the cusp of dreams, we sway,
Dancing along the Milky Way.
Stars above like lanterns gleam,
Guiding us through a starlit dream.

In this expanse, we spin and twirl,
As galaxies in whispers unfurl.
The pulse of time beats slow and sweet,
In cosmic rhythms, our hearts meet.

Celestial bodies, shining bright,
Illuminate the depths of night.
With every step, the heavens sigh,
As we reach out and touch the sky.

Nebulas bloom in colors bold,
Tales of ancient wonders told.
Across the firmament, we glide,
With starlit magic as our guide.

So let us dance on this astral stage,
In the chapters of the universe's page.
With every twinkle, we are free,
Dancing through eternity's sea.

The Night Sky's Gentle Narratives

The night sky holds its gentle tales,
In soft whispers as twilight pales.
Each star a word, each cloud a phrase,
In the cosmic book of endless days.

Beneath the firmament, we find our muse,
In the stories that the heavens choose.
With a brush of light, the sky unveils,
The dreams of time in silver trails.

In stillness deep, the light unfolds,
Guiding wanderers with heartbeats bold.
We listen close to the silent prose,
Of hope and love that gently grows.

From meteors that flash like fleeting thoughts,
To constellations mapping long-lost spots.
Each narrative weaves a golden thread,
Connecting hearts where journeys led.

So gaze above and let tales inspire,
For in the cosmos, there's always fire.
In the night sky's gentle embrace,
We find our truth, our sacred place.

The Undulating Glow of Wandering Light

In twilight's hush, the shadows play,
    A flicker here, a spark away.
With every step, the whispers sigh,
    As glowing orbs begin to fly.

They dance upon the shimmering stream,
    A fleeting touch, a waking dream.
Each luminous pulse, a tale untold,
As darkness wraps in twilight's fold.

In secret glades where magic weaves,
Among the boughs of ancient leaves.
The gentle glow of hearts in flight,
Enchants the world with pure delight.

Beneath the stars in velvet skies,
The wandering light, it softly lies.
A journey lost through nights of old,
A guiding flame, a hand to hold.

With every spark, a wish ignites,
In paths adorned by whispers' light.
The undulating glow, a shore,
Where dreams and stardust weave once more.

Secrets in the Crystalline Silence

In crystalline silence, whispers dwell,
A dance of shadows, secrets tell.
Each glimmering shard, a story spun,
Beneath the watchful, waning sun.

The frost-kissed air, a breath of night,
Where time stands still, enthralled by light.
With shimmering dreams caught in the frost,
The voices echo of love long lost.

A fragile peace where beauty sings,
Of ancient woods and magic springs.
Through whispered vows, the spirits tread,
In twilight moments soft and led.

The moonlight breaks, a silver seam,
Revealing all that once was dream.
Each winter's breath, a gentle sigh,
In crystalline silence, secrets lie.

When dawn appears, the magic fades,
Yet in the hearts, the spell cascades.
In every breath, the echoes cling,
And silence guards the truths we bring.

Celestial Moments Lost in Time

Amidst the stars, a path unfolds,
With every glance, a tale retold.
Celestial moments, bright and rare,
A dance of fate in evening's glare.

In cosmic tides, the dreamers play,
Where hours slip like grains of clay.
The whispers of the galaxy roar,
A symphony of evermore.

Through nebulae, the visions glide,
In silver boats on stardust tide.
Each fleeting spark, a heart's embrace,
In time's vast web, we find our place.

Yet shadows creep where light won't claim,
And sorrow sings a wistful name.
But still we chase that fleeting night,
For in our souls, we seek the light.

Though moments fade like softest sighs,
Their echoes linger in our skies.
In every heartbeat, hope will climb,
For love resides beyond all time.

Elusive Stars through Gossamer Veils

Through gossamer veils, the starlight gleams,
A tapestry woven of whispered dreams.
Each flickering spark, elusive glow,
Invites the heart to rise and flow.

Among the shadows, the secrets crawl,
In silvered light, we hear their call.
With every glance, a wish takes flight,
In the tender arms of the night.

Beneath the canopy of midnight's hue,
The cosmos paints its portrait true.
Each glinting orb, a distant light,
Guides wandering souls through winter's night.

Yet gossamer threads, they slip away,
When morning breaks, they cannot stay.
But still we chase the fleeting glow,
In every heartbeat, love will grow.

For even when the stars are lost,
And dreams are bound by twilight's frost,
The magic lingers in the fray,
Through gossamer veils, it finds a way.

Voyage Through a Canvas of Stars

Beneath a cloak of velvet skies,
Our spirits roam where starlight lies.
With whispers soft from cosmic streams,
We sail along on silver beams.

Galaxies spin in graceful dance,
We grasp at dreams in stolen glance.
Each twinkling light a tale unfolds,
In the silent night, our hearts are bold.

The fabric of the universe hums,
In every pulse, a promise comes.
We navigate through night's embrace,
And find our truth in time and space.

From comet tails to nebula's hue,
We chase the paths of the unknown, too.
With every breath, a wish we send,
To find the stars, our loyal friends.

So let us drift on this grand quest,
With open hearts, we'll find our rest.
For in each spark, the light will guide,
Through cosmic oceans, side by side.

Luminescent Memories in the Night Air

With fireflies dancing in twilight's breath,
We weave through shadows, cast by death.
Each glimmer holds a story sweet,
Of laughter shared and hearts that beat.

The moonlight bathes the world in gold,
A canvas where our dreams unfold.
We wander paths of silk and lace,
In every moment, find our place.

Whispers of the past swirl around,
In echoes soft, their voices sound.
Memories woven, light and dear,
A tapestry of love held near.

As stars adorn the midnight sky,
We gather moments, you and I.
In every breeze, a memory plays,
A luminescent dance of days.

So here we stand beneath the trace,
Of nights that time cannot efface.
With each heartbeat, we'll remain,
A symphony of joy and pain.

Celestial Riddles Amidst the Darkness

Beneath the shroud of night's deep haze,
Celestial riddles spark our gaze.
With every twinkle, questions bloom,
In the softness of the inky gloom.

What secrets does the cosmos keep,
In silent whispers, vast and deep?
Stars wink knowingly from afar,
Each gleam a puzzle wrapped in mar.

As comets blaze and shadows shift,
We ponder fate's peculiar gift.
In constellations' tangled threads,
Are woven dreams and words unsaid.

The night unfolds its mysteries grand,
Inviting us to take its hand.
What stories lie in starlit eyes?
A thousand worlds beneath the skies.

So we embrace this darkened sphere,
With wonder rising, casting fear.
In every riddle, strength we find,
Embracing truth for hearts aligned.

Glows of Forgotten Tales

In the twilight's hush, where shadows weave,
Are glows of tales we dare believe.
Whispers linger in the cool night air,
Each flicker tells of love and care.

Old stories echo in the breeze,
Of ancient lands and timeless trees.
Through winding paths and fields of gold,
The heart remembers tales retold.

With every star, a light ignites,
Illuminating lost delights.
Forgotten lore of hopes long past,
In starlit dreams, we hold them fast.

The gentle glow of memories near,
Reminds us of the things we steer.
We seek the wisdom in the night,
The solace found in faded light.

As dawn approaches, shadows blend,
Yet in our hearts, the tales extend.
In whispered songs of what once was,
We cherish glows, embracing cause.

Crystalline Trails of Astral Wonders

In the midnight sky they spark,
The stars begin their subtle dance.
Winding paths of silver arc,
Whispers of a dreamlike trance.

Each twinkle holds a tale untold,
Of ancient realms and magic fair.
Crystals gleam like thoughts of gold,
Floating softly on the air.

The night unveils its secret lore,
A tapestry of twilight's hue.
With every shimmer, hearts explore,
The wonders that lie just for you.

Through the cosmos, pathways weave,
Guided by the moon's soft light.
In dreams of magic, we believe,
Crystalline trails paint the night.

A journey through the dark profound,
With each step, the magic grows.
In the skies, new worlds are found,
As astral wonder gently glows.

Iridescent Shadows of the Cosmos

In hues of purple, blue, and gold,
The shadows dance in swirling grace.
Stories of the stars unfold,
In their embrace, we find our place.

Glimmers of a galactic stream,
Flowing through the inky deep.
In reflective pools, we dream,
Where secrets of the night do keep.

Among the stars that softly beam,
Mysterious, yet familiar sights.
In their whispers lies our theme,
Of journeys through celestial nights.

The cosmos sings a haunting song,
In every shadow, light does play.
Together, where the lost belong,
Iridescent night holds sway.

As we traverse the astral sea,
With every glance, our spirits rise.
In shadows, find serenity,
Beneath the vast, enchanted skies.

A Serenade to the Night's Glow

Beneath the arch of endless night,
Where starlight weaves its silken thread.
The world transforms in soft twilight,
Where dreams awaken from their bed.

A serenade of whispers sweet,
Calls forth the magic, bold and bright.
In moonlit paths, our hearts do meet,
Embracing all the endless night.

With every note, the echoes swell,
The melody of time and space.
In shadows deep, our thoughts do dwell,
Upon the stars, our souls embrace.

Each shimmer holds a tale divine,
Of love and hope, forever true.
In every pulse, the heavens shine,
A serenade for me and you.

Through silver mist, we gently glide,
Carried by the lunar glow.
In harmony, we shall confide,
A timeless dance, the night's soft show.

Pathways Paved in Silver Gleam

Along the paths of twilight's grace,
Silver threads of starlight weave.
With every step, we find a place,
Where dreams awaken, hearts believe.

The ground sparkles, a mystic glow,
Leading where the shadows play.
In every corner, magic flows,
Guiding us along the way.

Through ancient wood and whispered glade,
The silver gleam reflects our hopes.
With open hearts, we are not afraid,
For in this light, the darkness copes.

In lands of wonder, time stands still,
Each heartbeat flows with silver streams.
Together, let's ascend the hill,
And dance among our brightest dreams.

With every moment, feel the light,
For pathways paved in shimmering beams,
Unravel secrets of the night,
Where silver gleam fulfills our dreams.

The Secrets Held in Celestial Reflections

In twilight's hush, the stars awake,
Whispers weave through the moonlit lake.
Each ripple holds a tale untold,
Of ancient dreams and destinies bold.

Silhouettes dance in silver light,
Veils of shadows take flight in the night.
Crimson clouds drift, secrets spill,
A tapestry spun by the cosmos' will.

Echoes of time in stardust bloom,
Cascading wonders light up the gloom.
With every glance, a story unfolds,
The universe cradles the tales of the old.

Among the constellations, we search in vain,
For forgotten dreams that still remain.
In the silence of dark, our thoughts take flight,
The secrets held in celestial light.

So let us wander where skies embrace,
Discover the truth in this boundless space.
With hearts wide open, we shall believe,
In the magic that the starlit night weaves.

Horizon of Glowed Memories

At dawn's first light, dreams flicker awake,
Every heartbeat a wondrous mistake.
Golden rays weave through emerald trees,
Whispers of laughter on the soft breeze.

Footsteps echo on paths long gone,
Where memories glow like the rising dawn.
In every shadow, a story rests,
In the tapestry time has forever blessed.

With skies painted hues of tender past,
We chase the moments that forever last.
A horizon glows where hopes intertwine,
Reflecting a life, both yours and mine.

Upon the hills where silence sings,
We navigate through the joy life brings.
In twilight's embrace, let time stand still,
Our hearts aglow, dancing with will.

So here we stand with love as our guide,
In this realm where true wishes reside.
For every sunrise, a promise we greet,
Each memory cherished, ever sweet.

Chasing Lights along the Galactic Arc

Across the cosmos, where dreams entwine,
We chase the lights down the starry vine.
With every pulse, the universe calls,
A dazzling dance where starlight falls.

Through nebulous paths, our spirits soar,
Awash in wonders no heart can ignore.
Whirls of color, a celestial spark,
We follow the trails like a luminous arc.

In the depths of night, there's magic to find,
Galactic whispers flutter in kind.
Constellations guide us, steadfast and bright,
Chasing the echoes of pure delight.

With every leap, we break through the dark,
Charting our course with celestial mark.
In this infinite sea where wishes take flight,
We're weaving our dreams in the fabric of light.

So let us wander where the stars ignite,
In the dance of the cosmos, we find our might.
For every flicker ignites a new spark,
As we chase the lights along the galactic arc.

Mysteries of the Nebulous Path

In swirling mists of cosmological dreams,
We tread on paths where nothing is as it seems.
Each step a question, each breath a chance,
In the secrets that dance in the void's expanse.

Galaxies whisper their timeless lore,
Of wanderers lost and treasures in store.
Each nebula shrouded in colors divine,
Beckons the brave with a beacon's shine.

Through stellar gardens where wishes bloom,
We navigate shadows, unravel the gloom.
For in every corner, a puzzle awakes,
Holding the magic that reality makes.

So let curiosity guide our quest,
In this cosmic tapestry, we're truly blessed.
To explore the mysteries that call from afar,
Journeying deep to where wonders are.

Together we'll traverse, through night's gentle sway,
Unlocking the truths that the stardust relay.
For in this nebulous realm, adventures will last,
As we unveil the secrets of our past.

Trails of Luminous Wanderlust

Through forests deep, where whispers play,
A path of light leads dreams away.
With shimmering stars that gently gleam,
And magic woven in twilight's dream.

Each footstep dances on the dew,
Awakens secrets old yet new.
In every glimmer, an echo sings,
Of distant lands and wondrous things.

The moonlit trail, a guide so bright,
Illuminates the shrouded night.
With shadows cast by ancient trees,
On wind's soft breath, the soul finds peace.

By lantern light, desires unfold,
The heart's own compass, brave and bold.
In every nook where dreams reside,
The magic flows, the fears subside.

So wander forth, with care and love,
For the stars above are watching, too.
Each luminous trail beneath your feet,
Leads ever on, where wonders meet.

Cosmic Ripples across Twilight Fields

In twilight's grasp, the stars take flight,
Casting ripples of silver light.
Beneath the sky, a gentle sigh,
As cosmos whispers, time slips by.

Fields of dreams in radiant bloom,
Hold echoes of an ancient tune.
Each blade of grass, a story told,
Wrapped in magic, soft yet bold.

With every heartbeat, the cosmos calls,
In shimmering dance, the spirit sprawls.
The hush of night, an embrace so keen,
Invites the wanderer to be seen.

Among the stars, aspirations soar,
Past cosmic tides, to distant shore.
Where dreams converge and hearts align,
In twilight's grip, the worlds entwine.

So let the ripples guide your way,
Through starlit realms where dreams won't sway.
In endless night, your spirit's free,
To weave a tale of destiny.

The Celestial Wayfarer's Journey

Upon the road of endless skies,
The wayfarer treads where magic lies.
With each step taken on stardust ground,
In wonders vast, their heart is bound.

Through cosmic storms and radiant rays,
They wander forth in twilight's haze.
Through galaxies where dreams ignite,
Their spirit soars in boundless flight.

With maps of stars and whispers near,
Guided by love, not bound by fear.
They trace the paths of fabled lore,
In every heartbeat, they long for more.

Each moment held as a sacred tie,
As they embrace the night's soft sigh.
Through cosmic doors, their spirit gleams,
In endless space, they chase their dreams.

So journey on; the stars await,
With every breath, direct your fate.
For in the cosmos, you'll always find,
A place where heart and starlight bind.

Glowing Shadows on Ether's Edge

In the twilight's bend, the shadows glow,
On edges soft where secrets flow.
Beneath the stars that twinkle bright,
The ether sings of ancient night.

In every corner, a dream takes flight,
Casting silhouettes of sheer delight.
With glowing hints of journeys past,
The echoes linger; memories last.

Through veils of mist, the whispers call,
In tranquil peace, they rise and fall.
Each shadow dances, a tale to weave,
A tapestry of what we believe.

The edge of ether, a sacred place,
Where hopes and shadows softly trace.
In every flicker, a glimpse of grace,
Guiding the soul in its embrace.

So tread with care where shadows play,
For in their glow, the night turns day.
In glowing shadows, the heart will find,
The magic of the familiar kind.

The Heartbeat of the Night Sky

The stars whisper secrets, soft and bright,
A dance of light in the veil of night.
With every pulse, a story unfolds,
In twilight's embrace, a magic that holds.

From depths of darkness, a glow does arise,
A chorus of dreams beneath ancient skies.
The moon drapes her gown over hills so steep,
While shadows serenade the world into sleep.

In the silence, a heartbeat, steady and pure,
A promise that time will always endure.
For every wish upon a star's gentle light,
There lies a truth in the heart of the night.

So let the horizons of wonder expand,
With each loving whisper, a guiding hand.
In the heartbeat of evening, we find our way,
As starlit paths lead to the break of day.

Together we sail on this river of dreams,
Where night wraps the world in its shimmering seams.
With the heart of the night sky forever in sight,
We dance with the cosmos, entwined in the light.

Beneath the Canopy's Gentle Lullaby

In a forest where whispers cradle the leaves,
Magic awakens as twilight weaves.
Each breeze carries laughter, soft and sublime,
Beneath the green shelter, we float through time.

Shadows stretch long, in a playful embrace,
As fireflies twinkle with flickering grace.
A symphony hums in the heart of the wood,
Nature's sweet heartbeat, a language understood.

Lullabies echoed in the rustling trees,
The gentle persuasion of the night breeze.
With every soft sigh, the stars come alive,
In harmony cradled, our spirits revive.

The moon hangs low, casting silver's soft glow,
A guardian watching, through whispers of woe.
With each vibrant heartbeat, new tales will begin,
In the arms of the night, let the dreaming begin.

Under the canopy, lost in delight,
With friendship as endless as the vast night.
So let us wander where magic does lie,
Forever enchanted, beneath the night sky.

Moonlit Echoes Across Time's River

The river of time flows with whispers so clear,
Carrying secrets only moonlight can hear.
Fragments of laughter, of joy and of pain,
Each ripple a memory, each drop a refrain.

In the silver embrace of the shimmering night,
The past and the present unite in their flight.
Sailors of stars drift on moments long gone,
While echoes of hearts still pulse like a song.

Soft silken shadows waltz on the shore,
A dance of reflections, forever encore.
While dreams intertwine with the glow of the moon,
The river keeps flowing, a soft, gentle tune.

Every heartbeat resounds in the cool evening air,
A symphony rich with the tales that we share.
As time slips away, we cherish the night,
In the arms of the river, all futures ignite.

With memories weaving like threads through the dark,
The moon casts its spell, igniting the spark.
So let us remember as dreams drift and sway,
In moonlit echoes, let love light the way.

Winding Streams of Starlit Memories

Winding streams whisper with tales from the past,
In shimmering currents, forever steadfast.
Beneath a blanket of starlit embrace,
We gather the moments, the dreams that we chase.

With every soft wave, a heartbeat is shared,
Creating a tapestry, lovingly bared.
Fleeting reflections of laughter and tears,
Flow onward, transcending the bounds of our years.

Across gentle waters, the stars set alight,
As memories ripple in the hush of the night.
A dance of the ages, our stories unfold,
In winding streams bright, with wonders untold.

So let us find solace where waters collide,
In the embrace of the night, where our dreams can abide.
With each shimmering glance to the heavens above,
Winding streams flow with the warmth of our love.

Carried by currents through space and through time,
The stars keep our secrets, a reason to rhyme.
So here on this journey, let hearts intertwine,
As we sail toward horizons, endlessly shine.

Echoes of Ancient Light and Time

In shadows deep where whispers weave,
The tales of yore come to believe.
They shimmer like stars in the urban haze,
Guiding the hearts through forgotten maze.

From ruins old, a voice will rise,
It carries dreams through twilight skies.
Each echo holds a memory's glow,
Of battles fought and love's soft flow.

The lanterns flicker with memories past,
A tapestry woven, shadows cast.
With every heartbeat, the ancients sing,
Reminding us of the gifts they bring.

In quiet moments when time stands still,
We hear their laughter, feel their thrill.
The truths of ages brush our skin,
Inviting us back to where we've been.

So let us wander through ancient halls,
And heed the whispers in stone-cold walls.
For in each echo, a tale unfolds,
Of love, of magic, and legends bold.

Celestial Jewels on Night's Crown

The night unfurls her velvet cloak,
With diamonds strewn, a quiet joke.
Each twinkle whispers secrets rare,
Lighting paths through midnight air.

Constellations dance in harmony,
A symphony of tranquility.
Beneath their gaze, our dreams take flight,
Embraced by the charm of the silver night.

The moon, a guardian, watches close,
In her embrace, our wishes prose.
Each star a heart that beats with grace,
Reflecting tales of time and space.

In cosmic realms where magic stirs,
The universe writes its silent words.
With every blink, a story leaves,
Imprinted softly on souls' beliefs.

So lie beneath the starry art,
And feel their glow within your heart.
For in this solitude, we find,
The jewels of night, forever kind.

Aurora's Dance upon the Horizon

At dawn's embrace, the colors bloom,
A canvas bright dispels the gloom.
The sky ignites in vibrant hue,
As whispers of dreams begin anew.

With every brush, the heavens play,
A symphony of night and day.
The aurora twirls in graceful arcs,
Igniting hearts with its mystic sparks.

The world awakes to this grand display,
Where shadows bend and gently sway.
A tapestry of light unfolds,
As nature tells what time beholds.

In fleeting moments, the colors blend,
A promise whispered, love to send.
As daylight tips its hat with grace,
The dawn's sweet touch, a warm embrace.

So cherish each fleeting glimpse of light,
For in its glow, the world feels right.
Let auroras dance upon your soul,
And make your spirit whole.

Celestial Paths Through the Echoing Silence

In silence deep where stardust flows,
Celestial paths intertwine and grow.
They lead us forth through realms unseen,
To worlds where whispers build the dream.

Each star a beacon, guiding home,
Through the galaxies we freely roam.
The echoes of time, a gentle guide,
Awakening truths we cannot hide.

In the stillness, the cosmos speaks,
Of hidden wonders, mysteries unique.
Through every heartbeat, we draw near,
The universe wraps us in its cheer.

In twilight hours, when colors fade,
A dance of shadows begins to invade.
Yet in the dark, a spark ignites,
Illuminating all our flights.

So walk the paths where silence reigns,
And listen close to nature's pains.
For in the echoes of the night,
Our souls find warmth, and dreams take flight.

Murmurs of the Universe Underfoot

Beneath the stars, the whispers creep,
Of ancient tales the night must keep.
Soft winds weave through the emerald fields,
Where time in silence gently yields.

The earth, a canvas, worn and vast,
Holds secrets of the long-lost past.
Each pebble sings a song of lore,
A hymn that echoes evermore.

The roots entwine, a silent thread,
Connecting all the lives long dead.
From soil to sky, the stories flow,
In shimmering dreams that ebb and glow.

With every step, the magic stirs,
In whispers sweet, the universe purrs.
Feel the pulse beneath your feet,
A rhythm where the worlds do meet.

So listen close, with heart awake,
To the murmurs that the seasons make.
For in our souls, the echoes dwell,
Of mysteries none can truly tell.

Celestial Reflections in Tranquil Waters

In stillness lies the silver gleam,
A mirror held to every dream.
The stars above begin to sway,
Their light, like whispers, fades away.

With ripples soft, the secrets spread,
Reflecting thoughts that dance like thread.
The moonbeams dip in tranquil grace,
A guiding light, a gentle trace.

As shadows fall on glassy lakes,
The heart of night in silence wakes.
Each ripple holds a story clear,
Of love and loss, of hope and fear.

In quiet depth, the cosmos waits,
With every wave, the dream pulsates.
The universe in water's fold,
A canvas rich with tales untold.

So gaze upon this lovely scene,
Where stars and dreams have always been.
And in your heart let echoes flow,
In tranquil lights, let magic grow.

Embracing the Echoes of Twilight

As dusty hues embrace the night,
The world transforms, dimmed yet bright.
With whispers soft, the twilight calls,
In gentle tones, the daylight falls.

Embers of day fade to a glow,
Night's canvas dressed in shadow's flow.
Each fleeting moment, a velvet sigh,
As stars awaken in the sky.

With every breath, the silence grows,
In fields where softest twilight flows.
The echoes linger, sweet and low,
A serenade the stars bestow.

To hold this magic, pure and dear,
As dusk unveils what we can hear.
In every corner, a dream takes flight,
Embracing all that stirs at night.

So let the twilight whisper true,
Of mysteries that bridge me and you.
For in this spell, we find our way,
Through echoes soft, the close of day.

Journey Through the Galaxies of Thought

Within the mind, the galaxies spin,
A universe where dreams begin.
Each thought a star, bright and bold,
In swirling depths where tales unfold.

We drift through realms of vivid light,
In cosmic dance, both day and night.
With every idea, a comet flies,
Connecting hearts and distant skies.

Explore the depths of what you seek,
In silent moments, let thoughts speak.
For wisdom flows like rivers wide,
In cosmic spaces, we abide.

With every breath, adventures rise,
In starlit paths beneath the skies.
The universe within our reach,
In every lesson, life can teach.

So journey forth, with heart aligned,
To seek the beauty intertwined.
In galaxies of thoughts we soar,
A wondrous quest, forevermore.

Stardust Dreams In Twilight Fields

In twilight's grasp, where shadows play,
The stars do wink, they guide the way.
A soft breeze stirs the golden grain,
Whispers of magic in twilight's reign.

With every sigh, the night unfolds,
A tapestry of silks and golds.
Dreams drift softly on gentle tides,
Where each secret of heart confides.

In fields aglow with starlit gleam,
Night's embrace cradles every dream.
A symphony of sighs and stars,
As magic lingers beneath afar.

Beneath the moon's watchful embrace,
The world seems lost in a serene space.
Stardust dances on emerald waves,
In twilight fields, where silence saves.

So revel here in night's delight,
Where dreams unfurl and take to flight.
For in this place, hope softly beams,
Awake in stardust, live your dreams.

Ether's Glance on Twilight Roads

On roads of twilight, shadows stretch,
Where whispers dwell and secrets fetch.
The ether glances with a soft glow,
Inviting hearts to wander slow.

As stars ignite the inky sky,
Each path entreats a tender sigh.
Illuminated by dreams and lore,
Adventure calls from yonder shore.

Footsteps echo on cobbled stones,
A spirit dances with ancient tones.
With every step, the night awakes,
Beneath the moon, the magic breaks.

In twilight's arms, the world feels light,
Each breath of air, a pure delight.
The ether wraps around your soul,
As starlit visions take their toll.

Embrace the journey, let it flow,
For in your heart, the wonders grow.
Thus walk the twilight, hand in hand,
With dreams ignited in a twilight land.

Radiant Journeys Beneath the Night

Beneath the night, the journey gleams,
Each radiant path, a whispered dream.
Stars like lanterns light the way,
Guiding wanderers who long to stray.

Through fields of silver and moonlit streams,
Life unfurls like a tapestry of dreams.
With stardust kissed upon each face,
A dance of shadows, a soft embrace.

In gentle echoes of night's sweet song,
The heart finds where it does belong.
So take a breath, let spirits rise,
In radiant journeys, the magic lies.

The skies alight with colors bold,
Each moment captured, a story told.
With every heartbeat, the night unfolds,
A treasure wealth of dreams and gold.

So step with grace beneath the skies,
Where the moon bows low and hope replies.
For every journey, beneath the night,
Holds promise sweet in starlit flight.

Celestial Echoes in the Whispering Woods

In whispering woods, where secrets blend,
  Celestial echoes do softly send.
A melody floats on a gentle breeze,
  Lifting hearts with each wandering tease.

Among the trees where shadows twine,
  Mysteries dance in the moonlight shine.
The stars do twinkle with knowing smiles,
  Guiding souls over endless miles.

Through silver leaves with rustling sound,
  Magic abounds in this sacred ground.
Each step retells a tale of yore,
Where dreams take flight to the ancient shore.

The hush of night, a luring hymn,
  Inviting spirits to softly swim.
In celestial realms, our hearts unite,
  In whispering woods, oh what a sight.

So linger long where the wild things play,
  In nature's arms, let worries sway.
For the woods hold truths, both old and wide,
  In celestial echoes, let love abide.

Wanderings Under Astral Canopies

Beneath the stars, we softly tread,
Whispers of dreams, where shadows led.
With each step, a shivering sigh,
The cosmos beckons, calling high.

In glistening pools of silver light,
A tapestry spun, both fierce and bright.
We wander through realms, both near and far,
Counting our wishes on each bright star.

The wind carries tales of long ago,
Where magic lingers, hearts aglow.
Beneath the vault of endless night,
Each flickering flame ignites our flight.

Branches woven, in endless dance,
Cloaked in shadows, we find our chance.
In these wanderings, held so tight,
We embrace the wonder, pure delight.

With every heartbeat, the night unfolds,
Secrets of the universe it holds.
Under astral canopies, we roam,
Finding in starlight, a place called home.

Celestial Trails and Time's Embrace

In cosmic winds, where stardust flows,
Celestial trails, as memories close.
Time weaves a rhythm, soft and true,
In every heartbeat, a promise too.

Amidst the echoes of endless grace,
Time's gentle touch leaves no trace.
In the realm where wishes intertwine,
We dance through dreams, both yours and mine.

A flicker of light, a fleeting glance,
In the spiral of time, we find romance.
With every whisper of the night air,
We chase the shadows, nothing to spare.

Embraced by the heavens, we soar high,
Like comets painting the twilight sky.
In the fabric of time, our spirits race,
Celebrating life, in love's embrace.

Through celestial pathways, our journey flows,
In the heart of the cosmos, eternity glows.
Together, we wander, side by side,
On these trails of wonder, forever our guide.

Echoes of Light on a Moonlit Journey

With each step taken on silver beams,
Echoes of light awaken our dreams.
The moon, a guardian, watches near,
Guiding our hearts, erasing fear.

Soft whispers dance in the cool night air,
In this realm of magic, love lays bare.
The tapestry glimmers, woven bright,
A journey unfolds under stars' invite.

With lanterns glowing, we forge our way,
Each moment cherished, moments that stay.
In the stillness, we find our song,
Carried by night winds, we belong.

The path winds onward, a glowing thread,
Through shadows cast, where dreams are fed.
In the hush of night, our souls ignite,
Bound by the echoes of sweet moonlight.

With laughter's chime, we traverse the night,
A dance of shadows, a pure delight.
On this journey profound, hand in hand,
We trace our dreams across the land.

Dreams Woven in the Fabric of Night

In the quiet of dusk, where secrets lie,
Dreams are woven 'neath the velvet sky.
Threads of silver and strands of gold,
Stories of wonder, gently unfold.

As stars align, our visions gleam,
In the fabric of night, we dare to dream.
Each thread a heartbeat, each star a sigh,
Together we weave what never will die.

Velvet shadows caress our face,
In this woven realm, we find our place.
Illuminated whispers, soft and sweet,
Guide us through night on our wandering feet.

In the tapestry spun by moonlit gleam,
We share our wishes, like a flowing stream.
In dreams reclaimed, we rise anew,
In the fabric of night, we journey through.

With hearts entwined, as the night creeps near,
We gather the moments, precious and dear.
Within this realm, our spirits take flight,
In dreams woven deep in the fabric of night.

The Dance of Light and Shadow

In the twilight's gentle grace,
Shadows stretch and softly sway,
Whispers sing of fleeting time,
As night unveils its starry play.

Twinkling lights like scattered dreams,
Pierce the veil of midnight's gloom,
In their dance, a tale of hope,
And secrets of a moonlit bloom.

Each flicker holds our whispered wishes,
Carved in silence, soft as dew,
The dance of light, the pulse of night,
Revealing paths that feel brand new.

In shadows deep, the heart finds solace,
As echoes of the past resound,
Through the dark, we seek our way,
A sacred bond, forever bound.

As dawn approaches, colors rise,
The light breaks through the shadow's flight,
Yet in our hearts, the dance will linger,
A timeless waltz of dark and light.

Astrological Footprints in Soft Sand

On the shores where stars collide,
Footprints mark the cosmic tale,
Each grain of sand a memory,
Whispers borne on twilight's gale.

Beneath the sky, so vast and wide,
We trace the paths of distant spheres,
Seas of time, the ebb and flow,
Erasing doubts, dissolving fears.

Constellations guide our journey,
Constellations of love and fate,
In the dance of tides and twilight,
We find the magic that awaits.

Lunar phases mark our seasons,
As time drifts like the ocean breeze,
In the sand, our dreams take root,
A harvest sown with grace and ease.

So as the stars paint night afresh,
We wander where the cosmos flows,
With each soft step on endless shores,
Our astrological path bestows.

Celestial Paths of Forgotten Dreams

In the vast expanse of the night,
Where dreams reside and echoes stay,
Celestial paths like whispers call,
To those who tread the Milky Way.

Forgotten hopes like drifting stardust,
Paint the canvas of our souls,
Each flicker shines through time and space,
And binds us with celestial shoals.

We navigate the cosmic seas,
With hearts alight and spirits bold,
Through nebulous clouds, we seek the past,
In the stories waiting to be told.

Stars like lanterns guide our way,
Through memories that dance and twine,
Lost dreams invite us to explore,
To heal the scars with love divine.

As the universe expands and swells,
We walk the paths for which we yearn,
With each step, we breathe new life,
In cosmic rhythms, our hearts discern.

Stardust Cascades on Moonlit Shores

Beneath the gaze of silver moons,
Where waves embrace the whispering sand,
Stardust cascades in a gentle breeze,
A magical touch from a cosmic hand.

The ocean's pulse keeps time with stars,
In lullabies of night's sweet bloom,
As dreams drift softly on the tides,
To paint the dark in glimmers of plume.

We gather hopes like shells and pearls,
And weave them into tales of light,
Stardust pirouettes through the air,
A vision, vivid, pure, and bright.

Moonlight dances on the waves,
Kissing shores with shimmering grace,
In the starlit glow, our hearts awake,
Finding solace in this sacred place.

As dawn begins to softly break,
We hold the night within our souls,
In starlit whispers, dreams abide,
And cascades of love, our hearts console.

Whispers of Celestial Echoes

In the hush of night so deep,
Stars awake, their secrets keep.
Gentle sighs from worlds afar,
Echo softly, like a star.

Moonlight drapes the ancient trees,
Whispers float upon the breeze.
Ancient tales in shadows spoken,
Promises of dreams unbroken.

Mystic realms beyond our sight,
Guiding hearts through endless night.
In the silence, truth reveals,
Magic woven, fate conceals.

Across the sky, a flicker bright,
Time and space dance in the light.
Faint reminders of what's known,
In the night, we find our home.

Listen close to echoed lore,
In the dark, hear legends pour.
In the stillness, hope embodies,
Whispers of our cosmic bodies.

Twinkling Shadows on Midnight Trails

On the path where shadows play,
Midnight holds the dreams at bay.
Footsteps soft on dew-kissed grass,
Time stands still, as moments pass.

Stars above like lanterns gleam,
Guiding lightly through the dream.
Each rustle speaks of tales once told,
Of brave hearts and heroes bold.

Mysteries in the moon's embrace,
Whispers echo, time and space.
In the quiet, wishes grow,
Carried forth on winds that blow.

Underneath the silver glow,
Nature's symphony flows slow.
Creatures watch with eager eyes,
Twinkling shadows, ancient ties.

Through the night, a gentle song,
Melodies to which we belong.
In the darkness, hope ignites,
Illuminate our starry nights.

Beneath the Veil of Cosmic Dreams

Wrapped in starlight, dreams take flight,
Weaving visions, pure delight.
Floating softly on moonbeams bright,
Glimmers caught in endless night.

Whispers cradle the sleeping mind,
In the vastness, what we find.
Each twinkle tells a tale of old,
In shadows deep, our fears unfold.

Galaxies in swirling dance,
Where stardust offers sweet romance.
Harmony in every glance,
A tapestry of chance.

As the cosmos gently sways,
We are part of this grand ballet.
Fates entwined in silver threads,
While around us, magic spreads.

Beneath the veil, we dare to roam,
In the heart, we find our home.
Celestial echoes whisper clear,
In cosmic dreams, we draw near.

Starlight's Mosaic Across the Horizon

Upon the canvas, colors blend,
Starlight's mosaic knows no end.
Each flicker forms a vibrant hue,
Painting skies in depths anew.

Horizons stretch with endless grace,
Every star, a hidden place.
Glows of purple, silver, gold,
Stories whisper, yet untold.

Beneath the twilight's gentle sigh,
Wishes scatter, dreams will fly.
In the quiet, hearts unite,
Guided forth by soft starlight.

Ember clouds drift through the night,
Carrying secrets, pure delight.
Across the vast and boundless sky,
Hope awakens, soaring high.

In the evening's tender hold,
Magic weaves its tale so bold.
Starlight's mosaic, timeless art,
Illuminates the dreaming heart.

Shimmers of Hope Amongst Celestial Fireflies

In the twilight's gentle blink,
Stars awaken, soft and bright,
Whispers dance on the cool breeze,
Illuminating dreams in flight.

Hidden paths of silver glow,
Lead the lost through shadows deep,
With every pulse, a glint of grace,
Where hearts remember, and time can weep.

Flickering lights weave tales untold,
Of love and laughter, joy and tears,
Each firefly's kiss, a promise sweet,
To guide us through the length of years.

Hope's soft glimmer lights the night,
As doubts dissolve like morning dew,
Every shimmer a chance reborn,
A spark of strength to see us through.

Together, we rise, hand in hand,
With every wish cast upon the sky,
For even the darkest dusks will fade,
As fireflies whisper a lullaby.

A Journey Beyond the Veil of Night

Through the mist where shadows play,
A path unfolds beneath soft stars,
With hearts of courage leading forth,
To brave the night, our guiding scars.

The moonbeams weave a silken thread,
Magic swirls in the air we breathe,
Each step a tale, forgotten songs,
In the dark, we dare to believe.

On the edge of fright, we find our light,
Past mountains tall and rivers wide,
In dreams, we soar on wings of hope,
Past the limits where sorrows hide.

With every star, a wish is stored,
Each twinkle a story shared,
Together, we shall conquer fears,
With laughter echoing, love declared.

And when the dawn begins to break,
The veil of night begins to part,
For every journey's end reveals,
A new adventure - a brand new start.

Ethereal Lights Along Time's River

In the flowing stream of endless dreams,
Ethereal lights begin to bloom,
Rippling whispers of distant past,
Where memories cast away their gloom.

Tender hues of twilight fall,
As shadows dance in liquid grace,
With every pulse of time's embrace,
The river glimmers, a sacred space.

Along the banks where secrets lie,
Past stones that hum of tales once told,
Each spark a reminder of who we are,
In the warmth of the night, the air grows bold.

Through currents swift, our spirits glide,
Braving tides with dreams in tow,
While lanterns gleam above our heads,
Guiding us where the heartbeats flow.

And as the river whispers low,
Its journey woven, eternally clear,
We sail through time, hand in hand,
With every lantern, love draws near.

The Celestial Compass in a Sea of Stars

In the vast expanse of night,
A compass spins, adorned with starlight,
Through cosmic seas, our ship will glide,
Chasing dreams on this magical ride.

Planets twirl in a cosmic dance,
Guiding us with their radiant glance,
Each star a beacon, bright and true,
Leading us onward, me and you.

In the silence of the astral realm,
Our hearts align, like ships at the helm,
Through constellations, we weave our path,
In laughter and love, we find our math.

The Milky Way, a river wide,
Carries us forth on destiny's tide,
With faith as our anchor, hope our wing,
Through the heavens, together we sing.

For in this journey, ever bright,
The compass guides through darkest night,
With every star, our dreams take flight,
In a sea of stars, our spirits ignite.

Luminous Footprints in the Night

In silver grass, shadows softly sway,
Whispers of secrets from long gone days.
Moonbeams dance on the cold, dark ground,
Each step we take, a magic profound.

Stars blink brightly above our heads,
Painting dreams in inky threads.
Following the path where stardust leads,
With every heartbeat, the night concedes.

Footprints gleam, a trail of light,
Guiding our hearts through the velvety night.
Together we wander, alone we find,
The mysteries hidden in the folds of time.

A breeze stirs softly, a lover's sigh,
Cascading magic, soaring high.
With every turn a legend unfurls,
Between the stars, our dreams can twirl.

As night whispers all its gleams,
We follow fates woven from dreams.
With courage and love, we forge our fate,
In this realm where wonders wait.

Celestial Tapestry on Dusk's Canvas

A tapestry woven from dusk and dawn,
Golden threads as daylight is drawn.
Clouds cradle secrets, soft and sweet,
In twilight's embrace, where shadows meet.

Colors blend as stars ignite,
Crimson hues and shades of night.
Each stroke a story yet to be told,
By ancient hands both brave and bold.

Glimpses of magic whisper and peak,
Every heartbeat connects in mystique.
From the horizon, a spellbinding view,
A symphony of colors, a world anew.

Dancing shadows, they twine and weave,
In the soft hush where dreams believe.
Painting the sky from blue to gold,
While the heavens embrace, daring and bold.

As stars wake up, the night softly sighs,
Echoes of laughter in a sea of skies.
In this hallowed hour, we celebrate,
The celestial dance that holds our fate.

Glimmers of the Infinite Above

In the velvet sky, dreams softly glimmer,
With each twinkling light, our hopes grow slimmer.
Infinite tales in the dark we seek,
Finding the words when the silence speaks.

The universe whispers in echoes of night,
Guiding our souls with its timeless light.
Glimmers like lanterns on the shores of fate,
In this vast expanse, we contemplate.

With every pulse, galaxies spin and sway,
A cosmic dance that leads us astray.
Yet in each wander, truth lies unveiled,
A promise of light when darkness prevailed.

We trace the pathways where stardust flows,
With open hearts, we choose where to go.
Infinity beckons with a lingering spark,
In this wondrous night, we leave our mark.

As silence wraps round like an old friend's embrace,
We find our warmth in this endless space.
Among the glimmers, we dare to believe,
That from the infinite, we shall receive.

Chasing Nebulae Through the Darkness

In the heart of the night, where shadows collide,
We chase the nebulae, our spirits our guide.
Through the darkened landscape, dreams take flight,
Carving our stories across the night.

Every soft glimmer a promise anew,
Painted in colors of deep indigo hue.
Nebulae beckon with a voice so sweet,
Whispers of stardust beneath our feet.

With every breath, the cosmos expands,
We sail on waves crafted by timeless hands.
Among the wonders where starlight dances,
We find our path through fate's many chances.

Embracing the shadows, we forge our way,
With dreams interweaving, come what may.
Chasing horizons where magic unfolds,
In the heart of the night, our fate we hold.

Through the darkness, hope's light does shine,
With nebulae guiding, our spirits align.
Together we journey, past galaxies bright,
Chasing the beauty that blooms in the night.

Ethereal Threads of the Night Sky

In the hush of the midnight air,
Stars weave tales without a care.
Dreams alight on silver beams,
Whisper soft like ancient dreams.

Constellations dance in skies so vast,
Echoes of the present and the past.
Every twinkle, a story spun,
Guiding wanderers, one by one.

Moonbeams hang like delicate lace,
Illuminating the world's hidden face.
Night wraps gently in velvet folds,
Cradling secrets that night holds.

With each gust, the whispers sigh,
Stars blink softly in reply.
Threads of light weave through the night,
Creating shadows, soft and bright.

Underneath this sky, we find,
The threads that weave both space and time.
A tapestry of love and lore,
Forever binding evermore.

A Tapestry of Twilight Whispers

Twilight drapes in hues so rare,
Whispers linger in the air.
Colors blend like thoughts that flow,
In the quiet, dreams shall grow.

The world shifts as shadows fall,
Stars begin their silent call.
Every color shaped by light,
A tapestry unfolds in night.

Whispers linger, stories shared,
In this moment, hearts are bared.
Embers glow like distant fires,
Kindling poets' wildest desires.

Beneath the canopy, we stand,
Holding dreams with gentle hands.
Each star a wish, each sigh a hope,
Tangled threads, a fragile rope.

In the twilight's fading brush,
Thoughts emerge, creating much.
A silence settles, deep and sweet,
In this moment, life's complete.

Starlight's Embrace in Wandering Hearts

Wandering hearts seek the night,
Beneath a canvas, lit so bright.
Stars embrace, like lovers' hands,
Unraveling the cosmos' plans.

Dreams are painted in cosmic dust,
In the universe, we place our trust.
Every pulse, a heartbeat shared,
In this embrace, no souls are scared.

Whispers of hope on the breeze ride,
As dreams and journeys coincide.
The night is vast, yet close we stand,
Within the starlight, hand in hand.

With every flicker, love ignites,
Shining bright through endless nights.
Paths illuminated, spirits soar,
In starlight's glow, we are much more.

Every glance, a promise spun,
Wandering hearts, forever one.
Embraced by the night, we find our way,
In the starlight, we choose to stay.

A Mosaic of Dreams Under Moonbeams

In the quiet of the moon's soft light,
Dreams weave patterns, bold yet bright.
Each moment, a piece of art,
Scattered fragments of the heart.

Beneath the glow, we gather near,
Whispers float, so sweet and clear.
Moonbeams guide through the darkened haze,
A mosaic formed in fleeting days.

Every hope, a shining tile,
Creating paths for every mile.
In the silence, stories blend,
A timeless journey with no end.

As shadows dance with gentle grace,
We find our way through time and space.
Each dream a thread, each hope a gleam,
Together we create the dream.

In this mosaic, hearts align,
Bound by whispers, love divine.
Under moonbeams, we truly see,
The beauty of what we can be.

Starlit Whispers on an Endless Road

In the hush of night, secrets blend,
Twinkling lights where shadows extend.
Each star a promise, each breath a vow,
Whispers of dreams, in silence, we bow.

Winding paths through the velvet dark,
Footsteps echo, a wandering lark.
The moon keeps watch with a silver eye,
Guiding the hearts that dare to fly.

Time drifts softly on wings of grace,
Every moment, a sacred space.
The world dissolves in the starry sea,
In starlit stillness, we come to be.

Riddles of cosmos in shadows dance,
Cloaked in mystery, we take a chance.
The road extends, with wonders untold,
In starlit whispers, our dreams unfold.

Illuminated Secrets of the Night Sky

Beneath the stars, where silence reigns,
Stories linger, like soft, sweet strains.
Moonbeams weave through the dark, they flow,
Unraveling secrets that night may know.

Constellations flicker, old tales retold,
Guiding the lost with a touch of gold.
In this canvas, the heart takes flight,
Illuminated by secrets of night.

Echoes of laughter from distant lands,
A dance of dreams in celestial bands.
Every twinkle, a memory bright,
In the arms of the vast, we hold on tight.

The universe whispers, a tender sigh,
Secrets untold in the depths of the sky.
We wander, we wonder, beneath its embrace,
Illuminated truths in this timeless space.

Wading Through Galactic Dreams

In the deep of night, we plunge and glide,
Through cosmic waters, where wonders bide.
Galaxies swirl in a shimmering stream,
Wading through the fabric of a dream.

Stardust sparkles on waves of light,
Guiding our ships through the endless night.
With hearts as our sails, we journey far,
Navigating paths where wishes are.

Constellations shimmer, a map unfolds,
Stories of stargazers, brave and bold.
In the stillness, we find our way,
Wading through dreams as night turns to day.

Floating on whispers of cosmic tide,
We drift in wonder, our souls open wide.
In the depth of the universe's seams,
We find our truths in galactic dreams.

A Night Canvas of Cosmic Curiosities

Canvas of night, painted with grace,
Curiosities swirl in an endless space.
Each twinkling jewel, a question posed,
A tapestry woven, with secrets enclosed.

Whispers of comets in breezes dance,
Inviting the brave to seize a chance.
In shadows, the cosmos reveals its art,
Crafting connections that bind each heart.

Pulsating wonders in velvet skies,
In the silence, the spirit flies.
Each star a tale, each night a dream,
In this canvas, realities beam.

Embrace the mystery, let it ignite,
Curiosities lead to the stars' first light.
From dusk till dawn, in the silence we gleam,
In the night canvas, we live the dream.

www.ingramcontent.com/pod-product-compliance
Lightning Source LLC
Chambersburg PA
CBHW072350240125
20806CB00046B/960